Warrior Woman of Christ
Bible Study Journal

Kim Marie Johnson

SOMETHING BEAUTIFUL is about to happen...

Warrior Woman of Christ: Bible Study Journal

Design: Kim Marie Johnson

Cover Photo: Designed by Kim Marie Johnson

"Praying Hands" drawing by Artist, Albrecht Dürer; 1508

ISBN: 9781081202361

I am a
Warrior Woman for Christ

Introduction

I hope you enjoy this *Bible Study Journal*. It is a companion to *Warrior Woman of Christ: Find Your Armor and PUT IT ON Women's Bible Study.*

I know that there are those who say women are not warriors. They are so wrong. If you are ready to serve God, you must be ready to suit up and do battle with the father of lies every single day.

The only way to battle Satan is with the truth found in God's Word. The *Warrior Woman of Christ Bible Study Journal* provides ample space for the serious warrior to record important information about study passages.

Record the main theme of the chapter. List the people in the chapter, what they are saying or doing, and why they are important. There is a space for translations, footnotes, and definitions you may look up, and more. Most important are your own reflections, what you feel the Holy Spirit reveals to you, and its application, if any to your life.

God's Word is miraculous! After thousands of years, it is still relevant to us today. The truly amazing thing is you can read a particular chapter or verse many times during your life then, when you need it, God reveals its special meaning to you.

Tools of Bible Study:
- Bible
- Prayer
- Bible Study Journal
- Highlighter
- Fine tip pens
- A Willing Heart
- And a Hunger for God's Word

Extra Tools, you might find useful:
- Dictionary
- Bible Concordance
- Laptop or tablet
- If this is a group Bible Study, you will need sermon or lesson notes.

Bible

I believe the type of Bible you use is important. I personally use the King James Version. However, I also use my laptop to access on-line sites. Your computer, laptop, or tablet is fantastic for looking up other Bible Translations, Concordances, definitions, and sermon notes. Ask your pastor for online sites that are safe for this. You do not want to become bogged down and confused.

Some of the sites I use are:

- *www.biblegateway.com*
- *http://1611bible.com/kjv-king-james-version-1769*
- http://qbible.com/hebrew-old-testament/proverbs/31.html

Modern translations and the translations from the original Greek and Hebrew are very accurate. I think you will be surprised what you will benefit from these translations. On Bible Gateway. Type in one verse and when it appears, you will have the option to select "other English translations." This will then show all translations for you to compare.

Always look up footnotes when you study a chapter. Read the chapter through once. Then address each verse for more in-depth study. If the verse has Bible verses listed, it is important to look up these verses. This teaches us more about what we are studying and also helps us to understand the intricate way God's Word reveals itself to us.

Prayer

It is very important that we pray before we begin our Bible Study. Each time we prepare to study, we should begin by praising God. We should always ask forgiveness for our sins. We do not want unforgiven sins to keep us from close communication with God. Finally, we must ask the Holy Spirit to open our minds, our hearts, and our spirits to the understanding of God's Word.

Highlighter

You will want to highlight important passages in your bible. Your favorite color is fine. Alternatively, use more than one color.

Fine Tip Pens

If you write notes in your Bible, as I do, you will want to use fine tip pens. I use micro fine gel pens. I use black, blue, red and green. Predominantly, I use Black or red. However, if I have notes on a page and want to add new notes, I choose a different color to keep the sermon or lecture notes separate. Some people only use their pens to underline passages and that is fine. You must do what works for you.

Good luck in your study and God Bless.

"For we wrestle not against flesh and blood, but against principalities, against powers, against the rulers of the darkness of this world, against spiritual wickedness in high places. [13] Wherefore take unto you the whole armour of God, that ye may be able to withstand in the evil day, and having done all, to stand. [14] Stand therefore, having your loins girt about with truth, and having on the breastplate of righteousness; [15] And your feet shod with the preparation of the gospel of peace; [16] Above all, taking the shield of faith, wherewith ye shall be able to quench all the fiery darts of the wicked. [17] And take the helmet of salvation, and the sword of the Spirit, which is the word of God: [18] Praying always with all prayer and supplication in the Spirit, and watching thereunto with all perseverance and supplication for all saints;" (Ephesians 6:12-18 KJV)

My Bible Study Notes

Date _____ Book _____ Chapter _____

Central theme: or message:

_____

_____

_____

People in this Chapter

Person	Their Actions	Why Important to Know

Definitions I Looked Up

Verse	Word	Definition

Questions or Comments

_____

_____

_____

_____

Footnotes and Related Scripture I Looked Up

Scripture	What it Says	How it Relates

What I Learned

How Relevant to My Life

Verse (s) to Remember

Date _____ Book _____ Chapter _____

Central theme: or message:

_____
_____
_____

People in this Chapter

Person	Their Actions	Why Important to Know
_____	_____	_____
_____	_____	_____
_____	_____	_____
_____	_____	_____
_____	_____	_____
_____	_____	_____
_____	_____	_____
_____	_____	_____

Definitions I Looked Up

Verse	Word	Definition
_____	_____	_____
_____	_____	_____
_____	_____	_____
_____	_____	_____
_____	_____	_____

Questions or Comments

_____
_____
_____
_____

Footnotes and Related Scripture I Looked Up

Scripture	What it Says	How it Relates

What I Learned

How Relevant to My Life

Verse (s) to Remember

Date _____ Book _____ Chapter _____

Central theme: or message:

_____

_____

People in this Chapter

Person	Their Actions	Why Important to Know
_____	_____	_____
_____	_____	_____
_____	_____	_____
_____	_____	_____
_____	_____	_____
_____	_____	_____
_____	_____	_____
_____	_____	_____

Definitions I Looked Up

Verse	Word	Definition
____	_____	_____
____	_____	_____
____	_____	_____
____	_____	_____
____	_____	_____

Questions or Comments

_____

_____

_____

_____

Footnotes and Related Scripture I Looked Up

Scripture	What it Says	How it Relates

What I Learned

How Relevant to My Life

Verse (s) to Remember

Date _____ Book _____ Chapter_____

Central theme: or message:

_____

_____

People in this Chapter

Person	Their Actions	Why Important to Know
_____	_____	_____
_____	_____	_____
_____	_____	_____
_____	_____	_____
_____	_____	_____
_____	_____	_____
_____	_____	_____
_____	_____	_____

Definitions I Looked Up

Verse	Word	Definition
_____	_____	_____
_____	_____	_____
_____	_____	_____
_____	_____	_____
_____	_____	_____

Questions or Comments

_____

_____

_____

_____

Footnotes and Related Scripture I Looked Up

Scripture	What it Says	How it Relates

What I Learned

How Relevant to My Life

Verse (s) to Remember

Date _____ Book _____ Chapter _____

Central theme: or message:

_____
_____

People in this Chapter

Person	Their Actions	Why Important to Know

Definitions I Looked Up

Verse	Word	Definition

Questions or Comments

_____
_____
_____
_____

Footnotes and Related Scripture I Looked Up

Scripture	What it Says	How it Relates

What I Learned

How Relevant to My Life

Verse (s) to Remember

Date _____ Book _____ Chapter_____

Central theme: or message:

_____
_____
_____

People in this Chapter

Person	Their Actions	Why Important to Know
_____	_____	_____
_____	_____	_____
_____	_____	_____
_____	_____	_____
_____	_____	_____
_____	_____	_____
_____	_____	_____
_____	_____	_____

Definitions I Looked Up

Verse	Word	Definition
_____	_____	_____
_____	_____	_____
_____	_____	_____
_____	_____	_____
_____	_____	_____

Questions or Comments

_____
_____
_____
_____

Footnotes and Related Scripture I Looked Up

Scripture	What it Says	How it Relates

What I Learned

How Relevant to My Life

Verse (s) to Remember

Date _____ Book _____ Chapter _____

Central theme: or message:

_____

_____

People in this Chapter

Person	Their Actions	Why Important to Know

Definitions I Looked Up

Verse	Word	Definition

Questions or Comments

_____

_____

_____

_____

Footnotes and Related Scripture I Looked Up

Scripture	What it Says	How it Relates

What I Learned

How Relevant to My Life

Verse (s) to Remember

Date _____ Book _____ Chapter_____

Central theme: or message:

_____
_____
_____

People in this Chapter

Person	Their Actions	Why Important to Know

Definitions I Looked Up

Verse	Word	Definition

Questions or Comments

_____
_____
_____
_____

Footnotes and Related Scripture I Looked Up

Scripture	What it Says	How it Relates

What I Learned

How Relevant to My Life

Verse (s) to Remember

Date _____ Book _____ Chapter_____

Central theme: or message:
_____
_____

People in this Chapter

Person	Their Actions	Why Important to Know
_____	_____	_____
_____	_____	_____
_____	_____	_____
_____	_____	_____
_____	_____	_____
_____	_____	_____
_____	_____	_____
_____	_____	_____

Definitions I Looked Up

Verse	Word	Definition
_____	_____	_____
_____	_____	_____
_____	_____	_____
_____	_____	_____
_____	_____	_____
_____	_____	_____

Questions or Comments

_____
_____
_____
_____

Footnotes and Related Scripture I Looked Up

Scripture	What it Says	How it Relates

What I Learned

How Relevant to My Life

Verse (s) to Remember

Date _____ Book _____ Chapter _____

Central theme: or message:

_____
_____
_____

People in this Chapter

Person	Their Actions	Why Important to Know

Definitions I Looked Up

Verse	Word	Definition

Questions or Comments

_____
_____
_____
_____

Footnotes and Related Scripture I Looked Up

Scripture	What it Says	How it Relates

What I Learned

How Relevant to My Life

Verse (s) to Remember

Date _____ Book _____ Chapter _____

Central theme: or message:

_____
_____
_____

People in this Chapter

Person	Their Actions	Why Important to Know
_____	_____	_____
_____	_____	_____
_____	_____	_____
_____	_____	_____
_____	_____	_____
_____	_____	_____
_____	_____	_____
_____	_____	_____
_____	_____	_____

Definitions I Looked Up

Verse	Word	Definition
____	_____	_____
____	_____	_____
____	_____	_____
____	_____	_____
____	_____	_____

Questions or Comments

_____
_____
_____
_____

Footnotes and Related Scripture I Looked Up

Scripture	What it Says	How it Relates

What I Learned

How Relevant to My Life

Verse (s) to Remember

Date _____ Book _____ Chapter_____

Central theme: or message:

_____
_____
_____

People in this Chapter

Person	Their Actions	Why Important to Know

Definitions I Looked Up

Verse	Word	Definition

Questions or Comments

_____
_____
_____
_____

Footnotes and Related Scripture I Looked Up

Scripture	What it Says	How it Relates

What I Learned

How Relevant to My Life

Verse (s) to Remember

Date _____ Book _____ Chapter_____

Central theme: or message:

_____
_____
_____

People in this Chapter

Person	Their Actions	Why Important to Know

Definitions I Looked Up

Verse	Word	Definition

Questions or Comments

_____
_____
_____
_____

Footnotes and Related Scripture I Looked Up

Scripture	What it Says	How it Relates

What I Learned

How Relevant to My Life

Verse (s) to Remember

Date _____ Book _____ Chapter_____

Central theme: or message:
_____
_____

People in this Chapter

Person	Their Actions	Why Important to Know
_____	_____	_____
_____	_____	_____
_____	_____	_____
_____	_____	_____
_____	_____	_____
_____	_____	_____
_____	_____	_____

Definitions I Looked Up

Verse	Word	Definition
_____	_____	_____
_____	_____	_____
_____	_____	_____
_____	_____	_____
_____	_____	_____
_____	_____	_____

Questions or Comments

_____
_____
_____
_____

Footnotes and Related Scripture I Looked Up

Scripture	What it Says	How it Relates

What I Learned

How Relevant to My Life

Verse (s) to Remember

Date _____ Book _____ Chapter _____

Central theme: or message:
_____
_____

People in this Chapter

Person	Their Actions	Why Important to Know

Definitions I Looked Up

Verse	Word	Definition

Questions or Comments

_____
_____
_____
_____

Footnotes and Related Scripture I Looked Up

Scripture	What it Says	How it Relates

What I Learned

How Relevant to My Life

Verse (s) to Remember

Date _____ Book _____ Chapter _____

Central theme: or message:

_____
_____
_____

People in this Chapter

Person	Their Actions	Why Important to Know

Definitions I Looked Up

Verse	Word	Definition

Questions or Comments

_____
_____
_____
_____

Footnotes and Related Scripture I Looked Up

Scripture	What it Says	How it Relates

What I Learned

How Relevant to My Life

Verse (s) to Remember

Date _____ Book _____ Chapter _____

Central theme: or message:

_____
_____
_____

People in this Chapter

Person	Their Actions	Why Important to Know

Definitions I Looked Up

Verse	Word	Definition

Questions or Comments

_____
_____
_____
_____

Footnotes and Related Scripture I Looked Up

Scripture	What it Says	How it Relates

What I Learned

How Relevant to My Life

Verse (s) to Remember

Date _____ Book _____ Chapter_____

Central theme: or message:
_____
_____
_____

People in this Chapter

Person	Their Actions	Why Important to Know
_____	_____	_____
_____	_____	_____
_____	_____	_____
_____	_____	_____
_____	_____	_____
_____	_____	_____
_____	_____	_____
_____	_____	_____

Definitions I Looked Up

Verse	Word	Definition
____	_____	_____
____	_____	_____
____	_____	_____
____	_____	_____
____	_____	_____

Questions or Comments

_____
_____
_____
_____

Footnotes and Related Scripture I Looked Up

Scripture	What it Says	How it Relates

What I Learned

How Relevant to My Life

Verse (s) to Remember

Date _____ Book _____ Chapter _____

Central theme: or message:

_____
_____

People in this Chapter

Person	Their Actions	Why Important to Know

Definitions I Looked Up

Verse	Word	Definition

Questions or Comments

_____
_____
_____
_____

Footnotes and Related Scripture I Looked Up

Scripture	What it Says	How it Relates

What I Learned

How Relevant to My Life

Verse (s) to Remember

Date _____ Book _____ Chapter_____

Central theme: or message:

_____
_____
_____

People in this Chapter

Person	Their Actions	Why Important to Know
_____	_____	_____
_____	_____	_____
_____	_____	_____
_____	_____	_____
_____	_____	_____
_____	_____	_____
_____	_____	_____
_____	_____	_____

Definitions I Looked Up

Verse	Word	Definition
____	____	_____
____	____	_____
____	____	_____
____	____	_____
____	____	_____

Questions or Comments

_____
_____
_____
_____

Footnotes and Related Scripture I Looked Up

Scripture	What it Says	How it Relates
_____	_____	_____
_____	_____	_____
_____	_____	_____
_____	_____	_____
_____	_____	_____
_____	_____	_____
_____	_____	_____
_____	_____	_____

What I Learned

_____
_____
_____
_____
_____
_____
_____

How Relevant to My Life

_____
_____
_____
_____

Verse (s) to Remember

_____
_____
_____
_____
_____
_____
_____

Date _____ Book _____ Chapter _____

Central theme: or message:

_____

_____

People in this Chapter

Person	Their Actions	Why Important to Know

Definitions I Looked Up

Verse	Word	Definition

Questions or Comments

_____

_____

_____

_____

Footnotes and Related Scripture I Looked Up

Scripture	What it Says	How it Relates

What I Learned

How Relevant to My Life

Verse (s) to Remember

Date _____ Book _____ Chapter_____

Central theme: or message:
_____
_____
_____

People in this Chapter

Person	Their Actions	Why Important to Know

Definitions I Looked Up

Verse	Word	Definition

Questions or Comments

_____
_____
_____
_____

Footnotes and Related Scripture I Looked Up

Scripture	What it Says	How it Relates

What I Learned

How Relevant to My Life

Verse (s) to Remember

Date _____ Book _____ Chapter _____

Central theme: or message:

_____

_____

People in this Chapter

Person	Their Actions	Why Important to Know

Definitions I Looked Up

Verse	Word	Definition

Questions or Comments

_____

_____

_____

_____

Footnotes and Related Scripture I Looked Up

Scripture	What it Says	How it Relates

What I Learned

How Relevant to My Life

Verse (s) to Remember

Date _____ Book _____ Chapter_____

Central theme: or message:

_____

_____

People in this Chapter

Person	Their Actions	Why Important to Know

Definitions I Looked Up

Verse	Word	Definition

Questions or Comments

_____
_____
_____
_____

Footnotes and Related Scripture I Looked Up

Scripture	What it Says	How it Relates

What I Learned

How Relevant to My Life

Verse (s) to Remember

Date _____ Book _____ Chapter _____

Central theme: or message:
_____
_____

People in this Chapter

Person	Their Actions	Why Important to Know

Definitions I Looked Up

Verse	Word	Definition

Questions or Comments

_____
_____
_____
_____

Footnotes and Related Scripture I Looked Up

Scripture	What it Says	How it Relates

What I Learned

How Relevant to My Life

Verse (s) to Remember

Date _____ Book _____ Chapter_____

Central theme: or message:

_____

_____

People in this Chapter

Person	Their Actions	Why Important to Know

Definitions I Looked Up

Verse	Word	Definition

Questions or Comments

_____

_____

_____

_____

Footnotes and Related Scripture I Looked Up

Scripture	What it Says	How it Relates

What I Learned

How Relevant to My Life

Verse (s) to Remember

Date _____ Book _____ Chapter_____

Central theme: or message:

_____

_____

People in this Chapter

Person	Their Actions	Why Important to Know

Definitions I Looked Up

Verse	Word	Definition

Questions or Comments

_____

_____

_____

_____

Footnotes and Related Scripture I Looked Up

Scripture	What it Says	How it Relates

What I Learned

How Relevant to My Life

Verse (s) to Remember

Date _____ Book _____ Chapter_____

Central theme: or message:

_____
_____
_____

People in this Chapter

Person	Their Actions	Why Important to Know
_____	_____	_____
_____	_____	_____
_____	_____	_____
_____	_____	_____
_____	_____	_____
_____	_____	_____
_____	_____	_____
_____	_____	_____

Definitions I Looked Up

Verse	Word	Definition
_____	_____	_____
_____	_____	_____
_____	_____	_____
_____	_____	_____
_____	_____	_____
_____	_____	_____

Questions or Comments

_____
_____
_____
_____

Footnotes and Related Scripture I Looked Up

Scripture	What it Says	How it Relates

What I Learned

How Relevant to My Life

Verse (s) to Remember

Date _____ Book _____ Chapter_____

Central theme: or message:

_____
_____
_____

People in this Chapter

Person	Their Actions	Why Important to Know

Definitions I Looked Up

Verse	Word	Definition

Questions or Comments

_____
_____
_____
_____

Footnotes and Related Scripture I Looked Up

Scripture	What it Says	How it Relates
_____	_____	_____
_____	_____	_____
_____	_____	_____
_____	_____	_____
_____	_____	_____
_____	_____	_____
_____	_____	_____
_____	_____	_____

What I Learned

_____
_____
_____
_____
_____
_____
_____

How Relevant to My Life

_____
_____
_____
_____

Verse (s) to Remember

_____
_____
_____
_____
_____
_____
_____

Date _____ Book _____ Chapter _____

Central theme: or message:
_____
_____
_____

People in this Chapter

Person	Their Actions	Why Important to Know

Definitions I Looked Up

Verse	Word	Definition

Questions or Comments

_____
_____
_____
_____

Footnotes and Related Scripture I Looked Up

Scripture	What it Says	How it Relates
_____	_____	_____
_____	_____	_____
_____	_____	_____
_____	_____	_____
_____	_____	_____
_____	_____	_____
_____	_____	_____
_____	_____	_____
_____	_____	_____

What I Learned

_____

_____

_____

_____

_____

_____

_____

How Relevant to My Life

_____

_____

_____

_____

Verse (s) to Remember

_____

_____

_____

_____

_____

_____

_____

Date _____ Book_____ Chapter_____

Central theme: or message:

_____

_____

People in this Chapter

Person	Their Actions	Why Important to Know

Definitions I Looked Up

Verse	Word	Definition

Questions or Comments

_____

_____

_____

_____

Footnotes and Related Scripture I Looked Up

Scripture	What it Says	How it Relates

What I Learned

How Relevant to My Life

Verse (s) to Remember

Date _____ Book _____ Chapter_____

Central theme: or message:

_____
_____

People in this Chapter

Person	Their Actions	Why Important to Know

Definitions I Looked Up

Verse	Word	Definition

Questions or Comments

_____
_____
_____
_____

Footnotes and Related Scripture I Looked Up

Scripture	What it Says	How it Relates

What I Learned

How Relevant to My Life

Verse (s) to Remember

Date _____ Book _____ Chapter_____

Central theme: or message:

_____

_____

_____

People in this Chapter

Person	Their Actions	Why Important to Know

Definitions I Looked Up

Verse	Word	Definition

Questions or Comments

_____

_____

_____

_____

Footnotes and Related Scripture I Looked Up

Scripture	What it Says	How it Relates

What I Learned

How Relevant to My Life

Verse (s) to Remember

Date _____ Book _____ Chapter_____

Central theme: or message:
_____
_____
_____

People in this Chapter

Person	Their Actions	Why Important to Know
_____	_____	_____
_____	_____	_____
_____	_____	_____
_____	_____	_____
_____	_____	_____
_____	_____	_____
_____	_____	_____
_____	_____	_____

Definitions I Looked Up

Verse	Word	Definition
____	_____	_____
____	_____	_____
____	_____	_____
____	_____	_____
____	_____	_____
____	_____	_____

Questions or Comments

_____
_____
_____
_____

Footnotes and Related Scripture I Looked Up

Scripture	What it Says	How it Relates

What I Learned

How Relevant to My Life

Verse (s) to Remember

Date _____ Book _____ Chapter _____

Central theme: or message:

_____
_____

People in this Chapter

Person	Their Actions	Why Important to Know
_____	_____	_____
_____	_____	_____
_____	_____	_____
_____	_____	_____
_____	_____	_____
_____	_____	_____
_____	_____	_____

Definitions I Looked Up

Verse	Word	Definition
_____	_____	_____
_____	_____	_____
_____	_____	_____
_____	_____	_____
_____	_____	_____

Questions or Comments

_____
_____
_____
_____

Footnotes and Related Scripture I Looked Up

Scripture	What it Says	How it Relates

What I Learned

How Relevant to My Life

Verse (s) to Remember

Date _____ Book _____ Chapter_____

Central theme: or message:

_____

_____

People in this Chapter

Person	Their Actions	Why Important to Know

Definitions I Looked Up

Verse	Word	Definition

Questions or Comments

_____

_____

_____

_____

Footnotes and Related Scripture I Looked Up

Scripture	What it Says	How it Relates

What I Learned

How Relevant to My Life

Verse (s) to Remember

Date _____ Book _____ Chapter _____

Central theme: or message:

_____

_____

People in this Chapter

Person	Their Actions	Why Important to Know
_____	_____	_____
_____	_____	_____
_____	_____	_____
_____	_____	_____
_____	_____	_____
_____	_____	_____
_____	_____	_____
_____	_____	_____

Definitions I Looked Up

Verse	Word	Definition
____	_____	_____
____	_____	_____
____	_____	_____
____	_____	_____
____	_____	_____
____	_____	_____

Questions or Comments

_____

_____

_____

_____

Footnotes and Related Scripture I Looked Up

Scripture	What it Says	How it Relates

What I Learned

How Relevant to My Life

Verse (s) to Remember

Date _____ Book _____ Chapter_____

Central theme: or message:
_____
_____

People in this Chapter

Person	Their Actions	Why Important to Know

Definitions I Looked Up

Verse	Word	Definition

Questions or Comments

_____
_____
_____
_____

Footnotes and Related Scripture I Looked Up

Scripture	What it Says	How it Relates

What I Learned

How Relevant to My Life

Verse (s) to Remember

Date _____ Book _____ Chapter _____

Central theme: or message:
_____
_____

People in this Chapter

Person	Their Actions	Why Important to Know
_____	_____	_____
_____	_____	_____
_____	_____	_____
_____	_____	_____
_____	_____	_____
_____	_____	_____
_____	_____	_____
_____	_____	_____

Definitions I Looked Up

Verse	Word	Definition
____	_____	_____
____	_____	_____
____	_____	_____
____	_____	_____
____	_____	_____
____	_____	_____

Questions or Comments

_____
_____
_____
_____

Footnotes and Related Scripture I Looked Up

Scripture	What it Says	How it Relates

What I Learned

How Relevant to My Life

Verse (s) to Remember

Date _____ Book _____ Chapter_____

Central theme: or message:

_____
_____
_____

People in this Chapter

Person	Their Actions	Why Important to Know

Definitions I Looked Up

Verse	Word	Definition

Questions or Comments

_____
_____
_____
_____

Footnotes and Related Scripture I Looked Up

Scripture	What it Says	How it Relates

What I Learned

How Relevant to My Life

Verse (s) to Remember

Date _____ Book_____ Chapter_____

Central theme: or message:
_____
_____

People in this Chapter

Person	Their Actions	Why Important to Know

Definitions I Looked Up

Verse	Word	Definition

Questions or Comments

_____
_____
_____
_____

Footnotes and Related Scripture I Looked Up

Scripture	What it Says	How it Relates

What I Learned

How Relevant to My Life

Verse (s) to Remember

Date _____ Book _____ Chapter_____

Central theme: or message:

_____
_____
_____

People in this Chapter

Person	Their Actions	Why Important to Know
_____	_____	_____
_____	_____	_____
_____	_____	_____
_____	_____	_____
_____	_____	_____
_____	_____	_____
_____	_____	_____
_____	_____	_____

Definitions I Looked Up

Verse	Word	Definition
____	_____	_____
____	_____	_____
____	_____	_____
____	_____	_____
____	_____	_____

Questions or Comments

_____
_____
_____
_____

Footnotes and Related Scripture I Looked Up

Scripture	What it Says	How it Relates

What I Learned

How Relevant to My Life

Verse (s) to Remember

Date _____ Book _____ Chapter_____

Central theme: or message:

_____

_____

_____

People in this Chapter

Person	Their Actions	Why Important to Know

Definitions I Looked Up

Verse	Word	Definition

Questions or Comments

_____

_____

_____

_____

Footnotes and Related Scripture I Looked Up

Scripture	What it Says	How it Relates

What I Learned

How Relevant to My Life

Verse (s) to Remember

Date _____ Book _____ Chapter _____

Central theme: or message:

_____
_____
_____

People in this Chapter

Person	Their Actions	Why Important to Know
_____	_____	_____
_____	_____	_____
_____	_____	_____
_____	_____	_____
_____	_____	_____
_____	_____	_____
_____	_____	_____
_____	_____	_____

Definitions I Looked Up

Verse	Word	Definition
_____	_____	_____
_____	_____	_____
_____	_____	_____
_____	_____	_____
_____	_____	_____

Questions or Comments

_____
_____
_____
_____

Footnotes and Related Scripture I Looked Up

Scripture	What it Says	How it Relates

What I Learned

How Relevant to My Life

Verse (s) to Remember

Date _____ Book_____ Chapter_____

Central theme: or message:
_____
_____
_____

People in this Chapter

Person	Their Actions	Why Important to Know

Definitions I Looked Up

Verse	Word	Definition

Questions or Comments

_____
_____
_____
_____

Footnotes and Related Scripture I Looked Up

Scripture	What it Says	How it Relates

What I Learned

_____
_____
_____
_____
_____
_____

How Relevant to My Life

_____
_____
_____
_____

Verse (s) to Remember

_____
_____
_____
_____
_____
_____
_____
_____

Date _____ Book _____ Chapter _____

Central theme: or message:

_____
_____
_____

People in this Chapter

Person	Their Actions	Why Important to Know
_____	_____	_____
_____	_____	_____
_____	_____	_____
_____	_____	_____
_____	_____	_____
_____	_____	_____
_____	_____	_____
_____	_____	_____

Definitions I Looked Up

Verse	Word	Definition
____	_____	_____
____	_____	_____
____	_____	_____
____	_____	_____
____	_____	_____

Questions or Comments

_____
_____
_____
_____

Footnotes and Related Scripture I Looked Up

Scripture	What it Says	How it Relates

What I Learned

_____
_____
_____
_____
_____
_____
_____

How Relevant to My Life

_____
_____
_____
_____

Verse (s) to Remember

_____
_____
_____
_____
_____
_____
_____
_____

Date _____ Book _____ Chapter _____

Central theme: or message:
_____
_____

People in this Chapter

Person	Their Actions	Why Important to Know
_____	_____	_____
_____	_____	_____
_____	_____	_____
_____	_____	_____
_____	_____	_____
_____	_____	_____
_____	_____	_____
_____	_____	_____

Definitions I Looked Up

Verse	Word	Definition
_____	_____	_____
_____	_____	_____
_____	_____	_____
_____	_____	_____
_____	_____	_____
_____	_____	_____

Questions or Comments

_____
_____
_____
_____

Footnotes and Related Scripture I Looked Up

Scripture	What it Says	How it Relates

What I Learned

How Relevant to My Life

Verse (s) to Remember

Date _____ Book _____ Chapter_____

Central theme: or message:

_____
_____
_____

People in this Chapter

Person	Their Actions	Why Important to Know

Definitions I Looked Up

Verse	Word	Definition

Questions or Comments

_____
_____
_____
_____

Footnotes and Related Scripture I Looked Up

Scripture	What it Says	How it Relates

What I Learned

How Relevant to My Life

Verse (s) to Remember

Date _____ Book _____ Chapter _____

Central theme: or message:

_____

_____

People in this Chapter

Person	Their Actions	Why Important to Know
_____	_____	_____
_____	_____	_____
_____	_____	_____
_____	_____	_____
_____	_____	_____
_____	_____	_____
_____	_____	_____
_____	_____	_____

Definitions I Looked Up

Verse	Word	Definition
____	____	_____
____	____	_____
____	____	_____
____	____	_____
____	____	_____
____	____	_____

Questions or Comments

_____
_____
_____
_____

Footnotes and Related Scripture I Looked Up

Scripture	What it Says	How it Relates

What I Learned

How Relevant to My Life

Verse (s) to Remember

Date _____ Book _____ Chapter _____

Central theme: or message:

_____
_____
_____

People in this Chapter

Person	Their Actions	Why Important to Know

Definitions I Looked Up

Verse	Word	Definition

Questions or Comments

_____
_____
_____
_____

Footnotes and Related Scripture I Looked Up

Scripture	What it Says	How it Relates

What I Learned

How Relevant to My Life

Verse (s) to Remember

Date _____ Book_____ Chapter_____

Central theme: or message:
_____
_____
_____

People in this Chapter

Person	Their Actions	Why Important to Know

Definitions I Looked Up

Verse	Word	Definition

Questions or Comments

_____
_____
_____
_____

Footnotes and Related Scripture I Looked Up

Scripture	What it Says	How it Relates

What I Learned

How Relevant to My Life

Verse (s) to Remember

Date _____ Book _____ Chapter_____

Central theme: or message:
_____
_____

People in this Chapter

Person	Their Actions	Why Important to Know

Definitions I Looked Up

Verse	Word	Definition

Questions or Comments

_____
_____
_____
_____

Footnotes and Related Scripture I Looked Up

Scripture	What it Says	How it Relates

What I Learned

How Relevant to My Life

Verse (s) to Remember

Date _____ Book _____ Chapter _____

Central theme: or message:
_____
_____

People in this Chapter

Person	Their Actions	Why Important to Know
_____	_____	_____
_____	_____	_____
_____	_____	_____
_____	_____	_____
_____	_____	_____
_____	_____	_____
_____	_____	_____
_____	_____	_____

Definitions I Looked Up

Verse	Word	Definition
____	_____	_____
____	_____	_____
____	_____	_____
____	_____	_____
____	_____	_____

Questions or Comments

_____
_____
_____
_____

Footnotes and Related Scripture I Looked Up

Scripture	What it Says	How it Relates
_____	_____	_____
_____	_____	_____
_____	_____	_____
_____	_____	_____
_____	_____	_____
_____	_____	_____
_____	_____	_____

What I Learned

_____
_____
_____
_____
_____
_____
_____

How Relevant to My Life

_____
_____
_____
_____

Verse (s) to Remember

_____
_____
_____
_____
_____
_____
_____
_____

Date _____ Book _____ Chapter_____

Central theme: or message:
_____
_____
_____

People in this Chapter

Person	Their Actions	Why Important to Know

Definitions I Looked Up

Verse	Word	Definition

Questions or Comments

_____
_____
_____
_____

Footnotes and Related Scripture I Looked Up

Scripture	What it Says	How it Relates

What I Learned

How Relevant to My Life

Verse (s) to Remember

Date _____ Book _____ Chapter _____

Central theme: or message:
_____
_____
_____

People in this Chapter

Person	Their Actions	Why Important to Know

Definitions I Looked Up

Verse	Word	Definition

Questions or Comments

_____
_____
_____
_____
_____

Footnotes and Related Scripture I Looked Up

Scripture	What it Says	How it Relates

What I Learned

How Relevant to My Life

Verse (s) to Remember

Date _____ Book _____ Chapter_____

Central theme: or message:

_____

_____

People in this Chapter

Person	Their Actions	Why Important to Know
_____	_____	_____
_____	_____	_____
_____	_____	_____
_____	_____	_____
_____	_____	_____
_____	_____	_____
_____	_____	_____
_____	_____	_____

Definitions I Looked Up

Verse	Word	Definition
_____	_____	_____
_____	_____	_____
_____	_____	_____
_____	_____	_____
_____	_____	_____

Questions or Comments

_____

_____

_____

_____

Footnotes and Related Scripture I Looked Up

Scripture	What it Says	How it Relates

What I Learned

How Relevant to My Life

Verse (s) to Remember

Date _____ Book _____ Chapter_____

Central theme: or message:

_____
_____

People in this Chapter

Person	Their Actions	Why Important to Know

Definitions I Looked Up

Verse	Word	Definition

Questions or Comments

_____
_____
_____
_____

Footnotes and Related Scripture I Looked Up

Scripture	What it Says	How it Relates

What I Learned

How Relevant to My Life

Verse (s) to Remember

Date _____ Book _____ Chapter_____

Central theme: or message:

_____

_____

People in this Chapter

Person	Their Actions	Why Important to Know
_____	_____	_____
_____	_____	_____
_____	_____	_____
_____	_____	_____
_____	_____	_____
_____	_____	_____
_____	_____	_____
_____	_____	_____

Definitions I Looked Up

Verse	Word	Definition
_____	_____	_____
_____	_____	_____
_____	_____	_____
_____	_____	_____
_____	_____	_____

Questions or Comments

_____

_____

_____

_____

Footnotes and Related Scripture I Looked Up

Scripture	What it Says	How it Relates

What I Learned

How Relevant to My Life

Verse (s) to Remember

Date _____ Book _____ Chapter _____

Central theme: or message:

_____

_____

People in this Chapter

Person	Their Actions	Why Important to Know

Definitions I Looked Up

Verse	Word	Definition

Questions or Comments

_____

_____

_____

_____

Footnotes and Related Scripture I Looked Up

Scripture	What it Says	How it Relates

What I Learned

How Relevant to My Life

Verse (s) to Remember

Date _____ Book _____ Chapter _____

Central theme: or message:

_____
_____
_____

People in this Chapter

Person	Their Actions	Why Important to Know

Definitions I Looked Up

Verse	Word	Definition

Questions or Comments

_____
_____
_____
_____

Footnotes and Related Scripture I Looked Up

Scripture	What it Says	How it Relates

What I Learned

How Relevant to My Life

Verse (s) to Remember

Date _____ Book _____ Chapter_____

Central theme: or message:

_____

_____

_____

People in this Chapter

Person	Their Actions	Why Important to Know

Definitions I Looked Up

Verse	Word	Definition

Questions or Comments

_____

_____

_____

_____

Footnotes and Related Scripture I Looked Up

Scripture	What it Says	How it Relates

What I Learned

How Relevant to My Life

Verse (s) to Remember

Date _____ Book _____ Chapter_____

Central theme: or message:

_____
_____
_____

People in this Chapter

Person	Their Actions	Why Important to Know
_____	_____	_____
_____	_____	_____
_____	_____	_____
_____	_____	_____
_____	_____	_____
_____	_____	_____
_____	_____	_____
_____	_____	_____

Definitions I Looked Up

Verse	Word	Definition
_____	_____	_____
_____	_____	_____
_____	_____	_____
_____	_____	_____
_____	_____	_____

Questions or Comments

_____
_____
_____
_____

Footnotes and Related Scripture I Looked Up

Scripture	What it Says	How it Relates

What I Learned

How Relevant to My Life

Verse (s) to Remember

Date _____ Book_____ Chapter_____

Central theme: or message:
_____
_____

People in this Chapter

Person	Their Actions	Why Important to Know

Definitions I Looked Up

Verse	Word	Definition

Questions or Comments

_____
_____
_____
_____

Footnotes and Related Scripture I Looked Up

Scripture	What it Says	How it Relates

What I Learned

How Relevant to My Life

Verse (s) to Remember

Date _____ Book _____ Chapter_____

Central theme: or message:
_____
_____
_____

People in this Chapter

Person	Their Actions	Why Important to Know

Definitions I Looked Up

Verse	Word	Definition

Questions or Comments

_____
_____
_____
_____

Footnotes and Related Scripture I Looked Up

Scripture	What it Says	How it Relates

What I Learned

How Relevant to My Life

Verse (s) to Remember

Date _____ Book _____ Chapter_____

Central theme: or message:

_____

_____

People in this Chapter

Person	Their Actions	Why Important to Know

Definitions I Looked Up

Verse	Word	Definition

Questions or Comments

_____

_____

_____

_____

Footnotes and Related Scripture I Looked Up

Scripture	What it Says	How it Relates

What I Learned

How Relevant to My Life

Verse (s) to Remember

Date _____ Book _____ Chapter_____

Central theme: or message:
_____
_____

People in this Chapter

Person	Their Actions	Why Important to Know
_____	_____	_____
_____	_____	_____
_____	_____	_____
_____	_____	_____
_____	_____	_____
_____	_____	_____
_____	_____	_____
_____	_____	_____

Definitions I Looked Up

Verse	Word	Definition
_____	_____	_____
_____	_____	_____
_____	_____	_____
_____	_____	_____
_____	_____	_____

Questions or Comments

_____
_____
_____
_____

Footnotes and Related Scripture I Looked Up

Scripture	What it Says	How it Relates

What I Learned

How Relevant to My Life

Verse (s) to Remember

Date _____ Book _____ Chapter_____

Central theme: or message:

_____

_____

People in this Chapter

Person	Their Actions	Why Important to Know

Definitions I Looked Up

Verse	Word	Definition

Questions or Comments

_____

_____

_____

_____

Footnotes and Related Scripture I Looked Up

Scripture	What it Says	How it Relates

What I Learned

How Relevant to My Life

Verse (s) to Remember

Date _____ Book _____ Chapter_____

Central theme: or message:

_____

_____

_____

People in this Chapter

Person	Their Actions	Why Important to Know

Definitions I Looked Up

Verse	Word	Definition

Questions or Comments

_____

_____

_____

_____

Footnotes and Related Scripture I Looked Up

Scripture	What it Says	How it Relates

What I Learned

How Relevant to My Life

Verse (s) to Remember

Date _____ Book _____ Chapter_____

Central theme: or message:

_____
_____
_____

People in this Chapter

Person	Their Actions	Why Important to Know

Definitions I Looked Up

Verse	Word	Definition

Questions or Comments

_____
_____
_____
_____

Footnotes and Related Scripture I Looked Up

Scripture	What it Says	How it Relates
_____	_____	_____
_____	_____	_____
_____	_____	_____
_____	_____	_____
_____	_____	_____
_____	_____	_____
_____	_____	_____
_____	_____	_____

What I Learned

_____
_____
_____
_____
_____
_____
_____

How Relevant to My Life

_____
_____
_____
_____

Verse (s) to Remember

_____
_____
_____
_____
_____
_____

Date _____ Book _____ Chapter _____

Central theme: or message:
_____
_____
_____

People in this Chapter

Person	Their Actions	Why Important to Know
_____	_____	_____
_____	_____	_____
_____	_____	_____
_____	_____	_____
_____	_____	_____
_____	_____	_____
_____	_____	_____
_____	_____	_____

Definitions I Looked Up

Verse	Word	Definition
_____	_____	_____
_____	_____	_____
_____	_____	_____
_____	_____	_____
_____	_____	_____

Questions or Comments

_____
_____
_____
_____

Footnotes and Related Scripture I Looked Up

Scripture	What it Says	How it Relates

What I Learned

How Relevant to My Life

Verse (s) to Remember

Date _____ Book _____ Chapter _____

Central theme: or message:
_____
_____

People in this Chapter

Person	Their Actions	Why Important to Know
_____	_____	_____
_____	_____	_____
_____	_____	_____
_____	_____	_____
_____	_____	_____
_____	_____	_____
_____	_____	_____
_____	_____	_____
_____	_____	_____

Definitions I Looked Up

Verse	Word	Definition
_____	_____	_____
_____	_____	_____
_____	_____	_____
_____	_____	_____
_____	_____	_____

Questions or Comments

_____
_____
_____
_____

Footnotes and Related Scripture I Looked Up

Scripture	What it Says	How it Relates

What I Learned

How Relevant to My Life

Verse (s) to Remember

Date _____ Book _____ Chapter_____

Central theme: or message:

_____
_____
_____

People in this Chapter

Person	Their Actions	Why Important to Know

Definitions I Looked Up

Verse	Word	Definition

Questions or Comments

_____
_____
_____
_____

Footnotes and Related Scripture I Looked Up

Scripture	What it Says	How it Relates

What I Learned

How Relevant to My Life

Verse (s) to Remember

Date _____ Book_____ Chapter_____

Central theme: or message:
_____
_____

People in this Chapter

Person	Their Actions	Why Important to Know
_____	_____	_____
_____	_____	_____
_____	_____	_____
_____	_____	_____
_____	_____	_____
_____	_____	_____
_____	_____	_____
_____	_____	_____

Definitions I Looked Up

Verse	Word	Definition
_____	_____	_____
_____	_____	_____
_____	_____	_____
_____	_____	_____
_____	_____	_____

Questions or Comments

_____
_____
_____
_____

Footnotes and Related Scripture I Looked Up

Scripture	What it Says	How it Relates

What I Learned

How Relevant to My Life

Verse (s) to Remember

Date _____ Book _____ Chapter _____

Central theme: or message:

_____

_____

People in this Chapter

Person	Their Actions	Why Important to Know
_____	_____	_____
_____	_____	_____
_____	_____	_____
_____	_____	_____
_____	_____	_____
_____	_____	_____
_____	_____	_____
_____	_____	_____

Definitions I Looked Up

Verse	Word	Definition
_____	_____	_____
_____	_____	_____
_____	_____	_____
_____	_____	_____
_____	_____	_____
_____	_____	_____

Questions or Comments

_____

_____

_____

_____

Footnotes and Related Scripture I Looked Up

Scripture	What it Says	How it Relates

What I Learned

How Relevant to My Life

Verse (s) to Remember

Date _____ Book_____ Chapter_____

Central theme: or message:
_____
_____
_____

People in this Chapter

Person	Their Actions	Why Important to Know

Definitions I Looked Up

Verse	Word	Definition

Questions or Comments

_____
_____
_____
_____

Footnotes and Related Scripture I Looked Up

Scripture	What it Says	How it Relates

What I Learned

How Relevant to My Life

Verse (s) to Remember

Date _____ Book _____ Chapter_____

Central theme: or message:

_____
_____
_____

People in this Chapter

Person	Their Actions	Why Important to Know
_____	_____	_____
_____	_____	_____
_____	_____	_____
_____	_____	_____
_____	_____	_____
_____	_____	_____
_____	_____	_____

Definitions I Looked Up

Verse	Word	Definition
____	_____	_____
____	_____	_____
____	_____	_____
____	_____	_____
____	_____	_____

Questions or Comments

_____
_____
_____
_____

Footnotes and Related Scripture I Looked Up

Scripture	What it Says	How it Relates

What I Learned

How Relevant to My Life

Verse (s) to Remember

Date _____ Book _____ Chapter _____

Central theme: or message:

_____
_____
_____

People in this Chapter

Person	Their Actions	Why Important to Know

Definitions I Looked Up

Verse	Word	Definition

Questions or Comments

_____
_____
_____
_____

Footnotes and Related Scripture I Looked Up

Scripture	What it Says	How it Relates

What I Learned

How Relevant to My Life

Verse (s) to Remember

Date _____ Book _____ Chapter_____

Central theme: or message:

_____
_____
_____

People in this Chapter

Person	Their Actions	Why Important to Know

Definitions I Looked Up

Verse	Word	Definition

Questions or Comments

_____
_____
_____
_____

Footnotes and Related Scripture I Looked Up

Scripture	What it Says	How it Relates

What I Learned

How Relevant to My Life

Verse (s) to Remember

Date _____ Book _____ Chapter _____

Central theme: or message:
_____
_____
_____

People in this Chapter

Person	Their Actions	Why Important to Know

Definitions I Looked Up

Verse	Word	Definition

Questions or Comments

_____
_____
_____
_____

Footnotes and Related Scripture I Looked Up

Scripture	What it Says	How it Relates
_____	_____	_____
_____	_____	_____
_____	_____	_____
_____	_____	_____
_____	_____	_____
_____	_____	_____
_____	_____	_____

What I Learned

_____
_____
_____
_____
_____
_____
_____

How Relevant to My Life

_____
_____
_____
_____
_____

Verse (s) to Remember

_____
_____
_____
_____
_____
_____
_____
_____

Date _____ Book _____ Chapter_____

Central theme: or message:

_____
_____
_____

People in this Chapter

Person	Their Actions	Why Important to Know
_____	_____	_____
_____	_____	_____
_____	_____	_____
_____	_____	_____
_____	_____	_____
_____	_____	_____
_____	_____	_____
_____	_____	_____

Definitions I Looked Up

Verse	Word	Definition
____	____	_____
____	____	_____
____	____	_____
____	____	_____
____	____	_____
____	____	_____

Questions or Comments

_____
_____
_____
_____

Footnotes and Related Scripture I Looked Up

Scripture	What it Says	How it Relates

What I Learned

How Relevant to My Life

Verse (s) to Remember

Date _____ Book_____ Chapter_____

Central theme: or message:
_____
_____
_____

People in this Chapter

Person	Their Actions	Why Important to Know
_____	_____	_____
_____	_____	_____
_____	_____	_____
_____	_____	_____
_____	_____	_____
_____	_____	_____
_____	_____	_____
_____	_____	_____

Definitions I Looked Up

Verse	Word	Definition
_____	_____	_____
_____	_____	_____
_____	_____	_____
_____	_____	_____
_____	_____	_____

Questions or Comments

_____
_____
_____
_____

Footnotes and Related Scripture I Looked Up

Scripture	What it Says	How it Relates

What I Learned

How Relevant to My Life

Verse (s) to Remember

Date _____ Book _____ Chapter_____

Central theme: or message:

_____
_____
_____

People in this Chapter

Person	Their Actions	Why Important to Know

Definitions I Looked Up

Verse	Word	Definition

Questions or Comments

_____
_____
_____
_____

Footnotes and Related Scripture I Looked Up

Scripture	What it Says	How it Relates

What I Learned

How Relevant to My Life

Verse (s) to Remember

Date _____ Book _____ Chapter_____

Central theme: or message:

_____
_____
_____

People in this Chapter

Person	Their Actions	Why Important to Know

Definitions I Looked Up

Verse	Word	Definition

Questions or Comments

_____
_____
_____
_____

Footnotes and Related Scripture I Looked Up

Scripture	What it Says	How it Relates

What I Learned

How Relevant to My Life

Verse (s) to Remember

Date _____ Book_____ Chapter_____

Central theme: or message:

_____
_____
_____

People in this Chapter

Person	Their Actions	Why Important to Know

Definitions I Looked Up

Verse	Word	Definition

Questions or Comments

_____
_____
_____
_____

Footnotes and Related Scripture I Looked Up

Scripture	What it Says	How it Relates

What I Learned

How Relevant to My Life

Verse (s) to Remember

Date _____ Book _____ Chapter _____

Central theme: or message:

_____
_____
_____

People in this Chapter

Person	Their Actions	Why Important to Know
_____	_____	_____
_____	_____	_____
_____	_____	_____
_____	_____	_____
_____	_____	_____
_____	_____	_____
_____	_____	_____
_____	_____	_____

Definitions I Looked Up

Verse	Word	Definition
_____	_____	_____
_____	_____	_____
_____	_____	_____
_____	_____	_____
_____	_____	_____
_____	_____	_____

Questions or Comments

_____
_____
_____
_____

Footnotes and Related Scripture I Looked Up

Scripture	What it Says	How it Relates

What I Learned

How Relevant to My Life

Verse (s) to Remember

Date _____ Book _____ Chapter_____

Central theme: or message:
_____
_____
_____

People in this Chapter

Person	Their Actions	Why Important to Know
_____	_____	_____
_____	_____	_____
_____	_____	_____
_____	_____	_____
_____	_____	_____
_____	_____	_____
_____	_____	_____
_____	_____	_____

Definitions I Looked Up

Verse	Word	Definition
____	____	_____
____	____	_____
____	____	_____
____	____	_____
____	____	_____

Questions or Comments

_____
_____
_____
_____

Footnotes and Related Scripture I Looked Up

Scripture	What it Says	How it Relates

What I Learned

How Relevant to My Life

Verse (s) to Remember

Date _____ Book _____ Chapter _____

Central theme: or message:

_____

_____

People in this Chapter

Person	Their Actions	Why Important to Know

Definitions I Looked Up

Verse	Word	Definition

Questions or Comments

_____

_____

_____

_____

Footnotes and Related Scripture I Looked Up

Scripture	What it Says	How it Relates

What I Learned

How Relevant to My Life

Verse (s) to Remember

Date _____ Book _____ Chapter_____

Central theme: or message:

_____

_____

_____

People in this Chapter

Person	Their Actions	Why Important to Know

Definitions I Looked Up

Verse	Word	Definition

Questions or Comments

_____

_____

_____

_____

Footnotes and Related Scripture I Looked Up

Scripture	What it Says	How it Relates

What I Learned

How Relevant to My Life

Verse (s) to Remember

Date _____ Book _____ Chapter _____

Central theme: or message:
_____
_____
_____

People in this Chapter

Person	Their Actions	Why Important to Know
_____	_____	_____
_____	_____	_____
_____	_____	_____
_____	_____	_____
_____	_____	_____
_____	_____	_____
_____	_____	_____
_____	_____	_____

Definitions I Looked Up

Verse	Word	Definition
____	____	_____
____	____	_____
____	____	_____
____	____	_____
____	____	_____

Questions or Comments

_____
_____
_____
_____

Footnotes and Related Scripture I Looked Up

Scripture	What it Says	How it Relates
_____	_____	_____
_____	_____	_____
_____	_____	_____
_____	_____	_____
_____	_____	_____
_____	_____	_____
_____	_____	_____
_____	_____	_____

What I Learned

_____
_____
_____
_____
_____
_____
_____

How Relevant to My Life

_____
_____
_____
_____

Verse (s) to Remember

_____
_____
_____
_____
_____
_____
_____
_____

Date _____ Book _____ Chapter_____

Central theme: or message:

_____
_____
_____

People in this Chapter

Person	Their Actions	Why Important to Know

Definitions I Looked Up

Verse	Word	Definition

Questions or Comments

_____
_____
_____
_____

Footnotes and Related Scripture I Looked Up

Scripture	What it Says	How it Relates

What I Learned

How Relevant to My Life

Verse (s) to Remember

Date _____ Book _____ Chapter _____

Central theme: or message:
_____
_____

People in this Chapter

Person	Their Actions	Why Important to Know

Definitions I Looked Up

Verse	Word	Definition

Questions or Comments

_____
_____
_____
_____

Footnotes and Related Scripture I Looked Up

Scripture	What it Says	How it Relates

What I Learned

How Relevant to My Life

Verse (s) to Remember

Date _____ Book _____ Chapter_____

Central theme: or message:

_____
_____
_____

People in this Chapter

Person	Their Actions	Why Important to Know
_____	_____	_____
_____	_____	_____
_____	_____	_____
_____	_____	_____
_____	_____	_____
_____	_____	_____
_____	_____	_____
_____	_____	_____

Definitions I Looked Up

Verse	Word	Definition
_____	_____	_____
_____	_____	_____
_____	_____	_____
_____	_____	_____
_____	_____	_____

Questions or Comments

_____
_____
_____
_____

Footnotes and Related Scripture I Looked Up

Scripture	What it Says	How it Relates

What I Learned

How Relevant to My Life

Verse (s) to Remember

Warrior Woman of Christ

Becoming God's Woman

Look for Other Books in this Series.

Warrior Woman of Christ: Find Your Armor and Put it On!

Warrior Woman of Christ Praise and Prayer Journal

Becoming God's Woman—Unleashing the Secret Power of the
Proverbs 31 Woman

Becoming God's Woman—Praise & Prayer Journal

Becoming God's Woman—Bible Study Journal

Becoming God's Woman—Daily Agenda

Faith Filled—A Minister's Praise, Prayer & Reflection Journal

The Souled Out Youth Minister's Praise, Prayer & Reflection Journal

Joy Filled—A Children's Minister's Praise, Prayer & Reflection Journal

Called To Serve—A Young Man's Praise & Prayer Journal

Souled Out Youth— Praise & Prayer Journal

Visit my website at

www.kimmariejohnson.net

If you enjoy this journal, please leave comments on Amazon and our website.

We look forward to hearing from you!

Aggressively
Seeking
God

Becoming God's Woman

Learning to Recognize and Follow God's Plan for Our Lives

By

Kim Marie Johnson

Author and Speaker

www.kimmariejohnson.net

Watch for our upcoming Bible Studies

How To Bloom Where You Are Planted

Becoming God's Woman

This is My Shepherd

How To Renew Your Mind

Making It Personal

Forgiveness

Kim Marie Johnson is a speaker, author, artist, and designer. She holds a BFA in Interior Design from UGA. She enjoys speaking and teaching women's Bible studies. Most important to her are her relationship with God, her three children and five grandchildren who inspire her every second of every day.

organizer. She enjoys teaching and speaking. Most important